The Three Laws of Manifesting

by Kalyn B. Raphael

With Simon Townsen

The Three Laws of Manifesting

The Golden Flow System™ of
Accelerated Well-Being, Abundance,
and Enlightenment
http://lawsofabundance.com/

©2010 Lightwurks, LLC
All rights reserved by Lightwurks, LLC &
Kalyn Raphael & Simon Townsen

Dedication

I wish to express my gratitude

To my husband, Kris, who has always supported my passion

To our Ohana (spiritual family), who have always explored and discovered life and spirituality with us

And to our family and friends, who

Have all added love and joy to our lives

Thank you for being a part of the manifestations,
the dreams, we are living.

Introduction

Why is it that life seems to come easy for some and to be full of difficulty and frustration for others?

Isn't this also true in our manifesting?

Some people seem to have it all while others can't manifest what they need.

The biggest reason for this is because some people live out of the flow of life and others are in the flow because they live by the ***Three Universal Laws of Manifestation***.

What Is Manifestation?

For a minute, think about an ice cube, water in its solid form. When we add heat to the cube, it melts into water. Add more heat and the water then evaporates, or turns into a gas. In this state, the same elements, hydrogen and oxygen, raise into the sky—seemingly into the ethers.

As floating elements, the water particles can reverse and come back into a solid, physical state. They can come back into form as water or they can separate and re-form as anything that hydrogen and oxygen are composed of.

The same is true for all elements; when we reverse the above evaporation process, we can, and do, take energy to create something in our lives. We gather energy from the ethers and, as we activate the energy, the energy attracts elements. We thus begin to give it some form by bringing it into more and more solid states. Eventually, we then have a solid, physical experience, or a manifestation, that we encounter as our reality.

We all do this, knowingly or not. When we are in the flow of life, we tap into more power still with the help of our Source Energy (or what you may call your God, your Creator, Higher Self and so on). The trick in life, then, is to tap into the universal Laws which govern how manifesting works, as opposed to manifesting what we don't prefer.

In this book you will learn how manifesting can be done in three simple steps using:

1 - The Law of Self

2 - The Law of Attraction

3 - & The Law of Repetition

There are people who live according to these laws and live a happier, more fulfilling life. They experience more of what they wish to experience and have more of what they want.

Why not you too?

Manifesting is simple, the truth is that we do it all of the time. The trick is to use the *Universal Laws* that are required for us to manifest what we desire.

This book will take you through the simple steps to manifesting so that you can come to know these laws, how they work and how you can manifest using the flow of the Universe.

> ***"Is it not written in your law,***
>
> ***I have said, you are Gods"***
>
> **John 10:04**

The first *Universal Law* we need to use when manifesting is the **Law of Self.**

Most of the time many of us are not living by the Law of Self, but rather by the Law of Form, and this is a crucial correction we must make in order to become co-creators of our lives.

The Law of Form, can be the same for us all and it can be individual. This law is made up of the rules and beliefs of society or our upbringing. This Law will comprise systems that we each internalize based on what we have been taught at home, in school, in our religion or in our society.

For example, people often live by the cliché or belief that 'you have to work hard to get ahead'. They ignore the fact that there are people who get ahead with no effort at all, such as people born with money, people who "luck" into success or fame and fortune. In other words, we all know there are exceptions to any rule, but we tend to ignore the exceptions when they contradict our law or belief.

Given the choice, who would opt to work hard to get ahead if the choice to just be ahead were given? Is it wrong or bad to just be ahead? Is there something wrong with receiving an inheritance or a blessing of easy success or fortune?

Of course not. Some of you may believe that there is something wrong with this, that one does need to earn things in life. However, why would this be so? Is this what your inner self tells you, or is it something you have been taught?

This is what we mean by the Law of Form. This law dictates how life works, what we should think and believe; when and how we should love, work, play and so on. The difficulty with the Law of Form is that it is limited and inflexible. The Law of Form may dictate how we should live some of the time, but it cannot provide for every circumstance all of the time. It cannot speak to our individual experience and our individual needs. The Law of Form may dictate our doing, but it cannot address our being.

For example, if we did believe that we should work hard to get ahead or to earn our keep, then how could we truly *be* generous and tithe? How could we just give our money to someone else in need? Wouldn't they have to earn their keep too? Or is there an exception or a contradiction to this rule?

I want to make it clear that I'm not arguing any of these beliefs or rules. What you believe is yours, and it is not the belief or the rule that I am wanting you to see, but rather the Law of Form that you are living under.

The most powerful law that you can abide by is the Law of Self, as it comes from within and will not be based on inflexible rules or circumstances. The Law of Self is based on your Source Energy and you. It is about what is correct and true for you in the moment.

The Law of Self is about living in accordance to your true and authentic being.

Universal Law 1:

Living by the Law of Self

*"You are what your
deep driving desire is.*

As your desire is, so is your will.

As your will is, so is your deed.

As your deed is, so is your destiny."

Brhadaranyaka Upinishad IV, 4.5

A great TV comedy I enjoy watching is about two brothers. The show clearly illustrates the difference between living by the Universal Law of Self versus living by the Law of Form and it shows how different life is when we live by each.

The Show

The premise to this show is that two middle-aged brothers live together when the second, the Doctor, is broke after his divorce and needs a home. The first brother has always been single, is successful and lives in a beautiful home in Malibu.

The Musician

The older brother is a song writer who lives a debaucherous life but enjoys the lifestyle of a rich man. He does little work and still attracts a lot in life: women, work and money. He has a carefree, worry-free attitude in life, which his younger brother faults him for, arguing that the older brother has no values or morals.

The Doctor

The musician's life is contrasted with his younger brother's: a poor, divorcee who has no money even though he is a successful chiropractor. The younger brother, the chiropractor, is humiliated by life. This humiliation is furthered by his brother's life which lacks values and yet seems to be rewarded. The doctor leads a "good life", yet feels punished.

Law of Self or the Law of Form

The show illustrates an important *Universal Law* for us: we either live by the Law of Self or the Law of Form.

- Have you ever felt like things don't work for you even though they seem to work for others?
- Have you ever felt like "the rules" of life are different when it comes to you?

Well, like the doctor, you would be correct! They are.

People often sense, but then deny, the fact that life is actually very personal – our lives are designed specifically just for us to suit our energy and our individual purposes. Our lives are dictated by our own actions and life choices – we can choose to live by the **Law of Form** or by the **Law of Self**.

Although the musician's character is truly unhappy, he lives more by the **Law of Self** than the **Law of Form** because he makes decisions for himself. Under the **Law of Self** there is no reward/punishment system. If life were punishment-based, bad things would come to the musician regularly as a result of his gambling, drinking, womanizing and so on. Instead, because he considers his being and makes his choices based on himself, he lives in the flow of life. In this flow he is provided for and his more of his dreams come true.

The doctor, on the other hand, lives more so by the **Law of Form** as he tries to do the "right" thing and be a "good" person. By doing so, he is living according to how he thinks he should live (which has really been defined by society), instead of living according to his self. Under the **Law of Form** there is reward and punishment, which the Doctor experiences on a regular basis. The more he tries to be a good father, a good ex-husband, doctor or date, the worse things seems to go for him. He often expresses how lucky his brother is, regardless of his lack of deserving it, and how unlucky he himself is, regardless of how hard he tries to lead a good, respectable life.

What does it mean to live by the

Law of Self?

To live by the **Law of Self** means that we live connected to ourselves, to our authenticity and our being.

We know ourselves and we know what we need. We know what is right for us, whether it is viewed as right by others or not. Because we connect with ourselves in this way and make choices for ourselves we are connected to our Authenticity and, therefore, we are also connected to higher aspects of ourselves. We have chosen to truly act, feel and think for ourselves, leaving the doctor's world of disconnection behind.

*Living by the **Law of Self***

A quote from Kristopher Raphael, a coach & spiritual leader, about living from the **Law of Self**:

"On the spiritual side, there is the beautiful connection and love from unseen friends from other realms; on the human side there is the incredible love and connection with people. This is what it means to live by the Law of Self. You tap into these two realms and benefit from them both. You tap into your authenticity and you live the life of your dreams."

When we connect with ourselves in this way our lives change:

- We experience more synchronicities and more magic
- We are in Universal Flow

- We have an easier time making choices that benefit us so that we seem to have an easier time in life
- We experience more gratitude and joy in our daily lives
- We experience more connection with ourselves, with our Source Energy and with others
- We experience more love in all ways
- We manifest the life we truly desire more easily
- We experience more of the beauty that life has to offer

Although we still have challenges, we have stimulating challenges as opposed to painful ones.

A stimulating challenges, for example, may be taking on a new client in our own business. The client is impatient and may be quick to blame. They test our patience and our ability to make them feel like we are helping them. Nevertheless, we have attracted this challenge because we have lived by the **Law of Self** and have been able to start our own business.

On the other hand, had we been living by the **Law of Form** we would still be working for someone else. By working for another our challenge can be painful, not stimulating, as we are under our bosses thumb, which can be emotionally volatile. Our boss may be stern and inflexible so that we feel controlled and limited. We have fewer choices and our challenges are more painful since we live by the **Law of Form**.

Why do we experience more synchronicities and more magic under the Law of Self?

Let's look at the musician and the doctor again: because the musician is irresponsible and a big spender, he finds one day that he is running low on money and has run the course in his jingle business. The doctor is terribly worried about the musician's financial situation, since he depends on the musician for his well-being. He freaks out about the musician having so little money now and no money or jobs in sight.

The musician, on the other hand, is not worried about his financial situation and instead is irritated with the doctor's fears. The musician reassures the doctor that something will turn up and that they will be fine. Sure enough, with no effort on his part, a fluke babysitting job creates a whole new career for the musician as a children's entertainer. To keep his girlfriend's son occupied, the musician sings and records crazy songs for the boy. The boy takes it home to his father's, where the musician is 'discovered' by the producer-dad. In no time at all, the musician is swimming in money again – to the doctor's amazement.

People can live under different *Universal Laws* without being aware of it. The musician and the doctor are examples of this. The musician also demonstrates an excellent example of what it is like to live with synchronicities. Synchronicities come into our lives when we are aligned to our Source Energy. When aligned to Self, or our authenticity, we combine our ability to create our lives, which is limited, with our Source Energy's ability, which is unlimited.

The combination is powerful.

*How to Live by the **Law of Self**:*

In order to live by the **Law of Self** we need to connect with ourselves. The first way we do this is by connecting with our hopes, dreams and desires. This is one of the most powerful communication systems that our Source Energy uses with us, especially when we are in the first stages of developing connection.

Our deepest hopes, dreams and desires come from our Source Energy to guide us toward the fulfilling life that will bring us joy. Life is meant to challenge us, but it is preferable to be challenged by our dreams under the *Law of Self*, rather than by problems within the limited *Law of Form*.

The Unwelcome Fact

Without our Authentic Selves, at best, we only impact our lives by 20% (though the percentage is really much lower for many of us). This is an unwelcome fact to most people, but an important one when we are looking at manifesting. If we honestly look at our lives we will see that most of our life is not of our choosing – especially our major life problems. The truth is that everyone would change several things, at least, in their lives if they could.

We do have the ability to combine our own power to create with our Source Energy though, and this is what we are really after when manifesting. As we have said, our Source Energy communicates with us through our deep hopes, wishes, wants, dreams and desires (which we will just refer to as our dreams or desires). Manifesting these desires is fulfilling for us and it also connects us to our Source Energy.

The first thing we need to do in order to work on manifesting, therefore, is to tune into and connect with our own deep dreams and desires. This is an important part of the manifesting process and one that can be difficult for people who are disconnected from their dreams.

Tuning into our deep hopes, dreams and desires is a must when manifesting. This is the only way we can manifest in alignment with our Source Energy. This is also the only way to manifest with our Source Energy's 80% impact, greatly enhancing our creative ability.

Law of Self Process:

Focus on your hopes, wishes, wants, dreams and desires.

Spend some time over the next several days connecting with yourself and your dreams.

Don't let yourself feel like you are doing this wrong in any way – if you are connecting with what you prefer and dream of having in your life then you are doing it "right"!

This may seem simple, and it is. It is simple to connect with your Source Energy. But it is also powerful, so be certain to recognize that this simple task connects you with your Source Energy which has more power to create and manifest in your life. Whether it is simple or not, that connection, and those dreams, are what you are after.

Like The musician, choose to live by the **Law of Self** and tune into your true hopes, wishes, wants, dreams and desires for yourself. Use a journal to list all and any of your true dreams and desires.

Example of the Desire Process:

Here is an example of the desire process that one of the students went through in Kalyn's manifesting class. Notice that when she began the process, her desires were vague, and not as deeply connected to Self, or her authenticity. However, with guidance, she was able to tune into the energy at a deeper level, and find her true and authentic desire for her life.

Also note that as you journal or sit with your dreams and desires, welcoming them and connecting with them, you will automatically begin to deepen your desires on your own. Thus, it is important to connect with your dreams and desires often.

Rose: What do I truly seek? I feel that I seek a deep connection to my Self. What desire or wish from my list would most fulfill it? Music expands my emotional body[1]. It is my connection to Self that grounds me and also expands my awareness. The essence of music feels like love and joy that blaze with light. And that's how I feel when I am connected to my Self. How would that desire most fulfill it? Music is my connection to Self that grounds me and also expands my awareness. Music expands my emotional body. It's my touchstone. I experience the essence of music as love and joy that blaze with light. I want to go further with it, and bring it more into form.

Kalyn: A deep connection with Self is in your inner world. In your outer world a more direct reflection of that connection would hold a connection to people. You may choose to see if any of your desires involve connecting to people to deepen your level of fulfillment.

---

[1] Your emotional body is your feeling aspect; the part of you that perceives your life experience emotionally or through feelings.

Rose: Yes, I can see this. When I read this I had an Aha/light bulb moment. I need to sit with this. I know that a few of my desires with music relate to people, but I can go deeper to see what is there.

Thank you!

Rose: I've been observing music in me specifically with the inner and outer worlds and what a huge door to be opened and moved through. My inner world is already rich, deep and mostly satisfied but always hungry to grow. The outer world was cut off little by little until it really didn't exist for music. With my ego and wounding in control, there was no way in the past that I could find to bring music into my outer world that wasn't choppy and then abandoned because of misperceptions and fear. I have been pushing those experiences away.

I'm not finished yet with observing this in myself, and while it is much clearer what

I want to manifest in the outer world, I'm still not really zeroed in on the BE energy of it. But this is a huge AHA and I will work through it and get it. It brings me much joy to see that this is possible.

Thank you Kalyn!

Kalyn: What happened to your desire for a relationship? Wouldn't relationship give you the deepest connection in your outer world?

Rose: Yes, it would. I think I gave up. But I do have a strong desire. I'll tune into this.

Kalyn: Why would you give up on your desire?

When we give up on a desire and focus on something else, like music, then the something else can be a distraction and may not be fulfilling since there is a deeper desire at hand.

It's not to say that your music is not authentic, but because there is something deeper you will find that you would spend a lot of time and energy on music just to find that it would only lead you in the direction of the deeper desire.

If you are seeking something deeper within yourself then you will need to allow yourself to go deeper. You have been staying at a more surface level for some time, but going deeper and connecting is really the direction you will find your life and desires are pointing you in.

If you follow your true desires to go deep and connect then you will find greater fulfillment and color in your life - it would change and enhance your relationship to music as well!

Rose: Thanks Kalyn

I completely agree. It's time to go deeper and the desire for a relationship IS deeper. I was looking at my intent recently for being on an online dating site, and I saw that it wasn't clear. And it wasn't deep. I can and will correct that in my life. I'm excited to get going.

Thank you so much for steering me in this direction!

Refining Your Desire

In a class it is easy to help people deepen their desire, tapping them into the authenticity of it.

To do this, please be certain to spend time dreaming about what you desire. Whether you journal, share or explore your desire another way, spend time with the idea of what you are wanting. As you do, your dream will shift and change, deepening. Your dream will take on more authenticity and your Source Energy will have opportunities to enhance it within you.

The process of knowing what you are dreaming about and what you desire is powerful, so be certain not to rush this step. This is how you enhance your dream under the Law of Self. This is a way to bring more of your being and your authenticity to your dream, removing any beliefs, rules or ideas you may have otherwise imposed upon your dream due to the Law of Form.

Universal Law 2:

The Law of Attraction

"As you put out, so shall you experience. What we mean by this is that the energy you choose to be and experience in yourself is the energy that will be and that you will experience in your outer world."

- The Oracle

The 80/20 Rule

We are now entering phase two of our manifesting process. We have completed a difficult part by looking at what it is that our desires are and what, at a deeper level, we are really seeking and being guided towards. By spending time with our desires, we have found the desire that would most manifest what we are truly seeking.

We actually used a Universal Principal here too – the 80:20 principal. This principal states that we will get 80% of our output, what we are seeking, by 20% of our effort, or input. In other words, instead of wasting our time trying to manifest ten or even five things that were on our wish list, we will be more effective if we just focus on the 20% that will truly create the outcome we seek.

If we had tried to manifest all of the

desires on our list we would expend a great deal of time and energy to really achieve the same thing- the thing that we were really seeking and being guided towards. Instead, by taking the time to find the 20%, the one desire that most delivers what we are really after, we will be able to focus our time and energy in one direction so that we are more powerful, intentful and focused on our manifesting process.

The Law of Attraction

"Be the change you seek in the world."
-- Mohandes Gandhi

With our strongest desire now selected, we now turn to the creative processes to manifest in accordance to *Universal Laws*.

We will begin to use the *Law of Attraction* in order to attract what we are truly seeking.

The *Law of Attraction* dictates that, in the world of energy, we will attract the energy to us that we are. Physics uses the example of a tuning fork, which, when struck, only sets off other nearby forks that are the same key.

The energy that we are will attract similar experiences into our lives over and over, regardless of what we do to try to change this. Energy overrides form.

As another example, let's return to our two characters: No matter what the musician does he always attracts money, work and women because his own energy is more generous and confidant. In other words, because the musician has the energy of generosity he attracts money into his life; because he holds the energy of confidence his energy attracts lucrative work; and because he is confidant and knows what to say to women, he easily attracts beautiful women into his life.

The same is true of the doctor: the energy of his low self-confidant image attracts situations into his life in which he never gets ahead and only attracts women with a low sense of self-worth.

No doubt we can see this in ourselves: We all have had the experience of feeling like the same thing happens to us over and over, causing us to ask ourselves 'why does this always happen to me?'

The answer, of course, is that the same kinds of things happen again and again because we hold the same energy, attracting the same basic experience again and again. We may try to change our lives or the circumstances of our experience, but this does not work. Only changing our energy changes our experience, or our manifestation.

So, let's set out to change our energy!

An Example of The **Law of Attraction**

We will begin by using the Law of Attraction to BE what we wish to manifest. When we can shift our energy so that our beingness is the energy we want it to be, (for example, The musician IS generous) we will have taken our first step. To BE-come the energy we want to be we first need to hold the beingness in ourselves, which we can do by beginning to recognize it as ourselves. Simply put, we need to find this BE-ingness in our lives now.

Example:
I want to BE a caring mother.

Now I need to find ways in which it is already present in my life both in energy and in form.

I can begin by recognizing that I have a

deep love for my daughter and I truly want to do right by her. I will look to myself and my life to find places where I have made choices that were beneficial for her, when I have taken care of her. I won't focus on times when I have not… instead I look to how and when I did meet her needs. I see how it helped her develop in a healthy way – even if I had only met her need one time so far. It may be that I feel I need to focus on her a lot more to be a caring mother. But at least I now know what to focus on and see that it is present in my life, I just need to increase this. Next I may look at the time I spend with her. If I feel that it would benefit her to have a lot of my time dedicated to her, but it is hard because I am busy cooking, cleaning and so on, then I need to find times when I have dedicated my time and attention to her. Again, there may not be many times when I have dedicated time to her, but if I find just one then this means that I have the energy within me.

Now I have found that I have the energy of BE-ing a caring mother: caring for her and spending time with her.

The point of this exercise is not to have us dig through our past for times when we have done the "right" thing- the point is to recognize that since the desire is in us then the ability to manifest it is too. Not only is the ability to manifest it within us, but we really are creating a reference point for ourselves that shows us that we can manifest what we desire and experience this. It will be our choice to choose to be what we desire every day if we wish to experience the manifestation permanently in our lives (as opposed to only experiencing it every now and then when it manifests without our intent).

Be that which you wish to manifest,

Be-come that which you wish to experience &

Be-lieve that which you wisht to live~

The Oracle

An important detail to notice when manifesting:

Many people think that if they had something, like money, then they would be able to manifest joy in their lives, since they could then afford to relax and take a trip. However, this is not the way manifestation works. Often, the right circumstances never present themselves when we wait for life to change instead of changing ourselves or our energy.

In order to manifest what we desire, we need to imagine what it would be like to have our desire fulfilled. We need to do our best to bring the joy into our lives first, to be joyful. This will then attract the energy of what we desire, manifesting the money in this example.

*The **Law of Attraction** Process:*

"Things do not change, we change."
-- Henry David Thoreau

For the next week connect with the energy you want to BE-come, the energy or feeling of your desire.

Start by finding the energy in your life now, tapping you into the power of the now moment.

After you have found the energy in your life, tap into the energy any way you like on a daily basis:

- Recall your desire often by keeping something (a photo, an object) that holds the energy or feeling for you
- Talk about your dream with your friends
- Journal about your dream
- Research your dream

- Dream about what it will be like to experience your dream
- Explore how your life will change with your dream fulfilled
- Explore who will be with you in your dream and what you will do

*An example of the **Law of Attraction:***

Here is an example of a student first listing his desires, then tuning into the energy, finding what he truly seeks, and beginning to align to that energy.

George: Right off the top I want to manifest:

> · More money, lots of money, money that would bring me stability, and the ability to help others, like my granddaughters, I would like to give them a full and varied education throughout their lives.
>
> · More time, time to spend in pursuits like learning to play the

guitar, time to meditate and work on myself and just down time.

·   More living space, a bigger home with land away from the urban centre.

·   A motorcycle, a mid-sized cruiser, just because.

·   A friend, someone that I can really connect to. A man close to my age that I can share my thoughts and spiritual life with.

·   I would like to manifest a feeling of satisfaction in my life. A feeling that I am doing well, a feeling of happiness.

Kalyn: George: 1) What do you truly seek

2) What desire or wish do you feel would most fulfill that which

you seek?

3) How would that desire most fulfill it?

George: What I truly seek is Freedom.

My first desire – more money – seems to me to fulfill my desire for freedom the best. If I had greater abundance in my life, most of my other desires would come easily.

If I had more abundance I would have fewer restrictions: on my time, space, ability to do things I want and I would be able to make choices with greater freedom.

Kalyn: I commend the energy and intent you have towards realizing your desires, but I need to bring to your attention the choice you are making that is outside of our manifesting process. You have chosen what you perceive to be a representation of freedom and are looking at buying a bike. This bypasses our process: we are committing to our desires; this is inner world work. Yours is an outer world action that may or may not be in alignment to your desire.

In the next lesson we will start to find an inner world representation of our desire, for you this might be finding a photograph of a motorcycle if that, to you, captures the essence of freedom. As I understood you, you were seeking freedom from your conditioning that kept your from making your own authentic choices. It is not clear how a motorcycle frees you from your conditioning; however, it can represent escape. Be careful not to allow ego to be the one making choices or taking actions.

If you stick with the process you may find that purchasing a motorcycle is not what you really want or need; follow the process and it will shift your energy, your perception and empower you to make beneficial changes that enhance your manifesting process.

George: Hi Kalyn,
I have sat with the above for many days now. At first it was a real blow to me, but now, I see it only as a blow to my ego. In searching my inner world for images that represent freedom I

see that a motorcycle is just a cheap imitation of what I really want. It is a band-aid solution that is born of ego. This does not mean that I will not own a motorcycle at some point, but for now it would derail this process, and I see that.

When I first read your post I felt that I could never accept what you said but I made myself read it over and over. I felt it in my being until I could feel the veracity in your words. Today I have a new image of freedom in my head, even though this too may pass, it is closer to what I really want.

Thank you for your words.

George: Just today I connected

with a time that I felt free and abundant…and happy, excited about life. I will hold this image and recall it often.

Kalyn: Awesome, George!

Do continue to connect with that time and energy over and over.

Universal Law 3:

The Law of Repetition

"Inherit in every intention and desire is the mechanism for its fulfillment."

- Deepak Chopra

Rituals & **The Law of Repetition**

Being Who You Are:

One of the most difficult parts of manifesting is BE-ing who you really are. This means that it tends to be very difficult for people to shift their behavior, their habits and their daily rituals, just because they are routine.

However, in order to manifest your desires, you must be the person with your desires. You must find the version of you that has changed positively as a result of having of your dream fulfilled.

For example, if you desire a relationship, then you will manifest it when you create a new habit of opening to others and connecting with them. Your old habit of spending time alone needs to be left behind.

Since we have years and years of behaving from ego, we have mastered ego-based thoughts, feelings and behaviors – most importantly – we have mastered ego-based energies too. At first these took effort, but now that we have mastered being ego-based, behaving from ego is just what we do. We don't even have to try, it is by default.

Everyone knows how to drive a car and, chances are, you don't think about your driving when you do. You are on auto-pilot because a part of you automatically takes over and drives safely. You have mastered driving.

The same is true of ourselves in our lives: we are going through life with our egos in the driver's seat. We don't even pay attention to how ego 'drives' because it is simply a life-long habit, just like when we drive our cars.

We can change all of this!

We can take over and let our authentic selves 'drive' our lives! Our authentic selves can manifest, and quickly, when in the driver's seat.

The way to change your habits or old behaviors is by creating new ones so that you are using the Law of Repetition in your creation.

Step by Step Process:

What we need to do:

1. Choose to take over the steering wheel every day (and as often throughout the day as possible)
2. Choose what we want to manifest in our lives
3. Being: Be-come the energy of this as best we can
4. Doing: Find the aligned thoughts
5. Doing: Find the aligned feelings
6. Doing: Find the actions

Choosing the aligned being and doing for ourselves is choosing to put our authentic selves in charge of our lives and our manifestations.

Habitual Energy Vs Energy of Your Desires

Let's re-visit our example of the doctor from the TV show one more time.

He doesn't make aligned choices every day. With his ego at the driver's seat, the doctor often stops himself from speaking to beautiful women, for example, since he knows (belief) that he will just be rejected anyway (low self-worth). Notice that his belief and low self-worth come from the Law of Form, which says he's a loser and which he never contests.

So, every day when he wakes up he comes from an energy which is limited and that won't open to new possibilities since he feels there is no point in trying, just to be disappointed again. His ego-based personality has set up behaviors and attitudes that keep the doctor subdued and certain that his dreams could never come true.

Now if the doctor were to decide to let his authentic self take the driver's seat, then he would wake up every morning and do things differently.

First, he would feel differently, waking up with enthusiasm for something, anything, in his day.

He would tap into his desire to improve his self-worth and he would align to it. Perhaps he could do this by focusing on the help he offers his clients as a doctor.

If he chose to manifest a joyful day for himself, he could do things like play music that is uplifting to him at work, do some on-line dating and meeting new friends. Partaking in these new behaviors would tap the doctor into the Law of Repetition, which would bring the energy and experience of a joyful and confident version of himself forward.

When he puts his intent into what he wishes to manifest on a daily basis then his life will change and he will manifest his true desire.

Also, at this point the doctor will be more open, welcoming and apt to attract women into his life.

———

The Law of Repetition

It is important to be determined to put the energy into what you wish to manifest every day. At first when we are creating something new we are starting from scratch, which means there is nothing there. Just like building a house where there is first only a pile of dirt, we need to bring materials to build the foundation. Then we need more materials to lay the electric and plumbing down. Then we need more materials to build the frame. Then we need more materials to begin to create walls. Then… get the point? To build anything in form we have to keep at it. We bring what it needs over and over. This is using the Law of Repetition.

The doctor finds a song that pumps him up in the morning and taps him into a small aspect of his personality that is more confidant and expressive. The song puts him in touch with this part of self, which has far more self-worth than the "normal" doctor. By listening to it every morning with the intent of brining this energy of the confidant self and then brining the alignment of this confidant self to him, the doctor creates a ritual.

The ritual, when done over and over again, begins to build in energy and, in time, it begins to really feed the doctor. His energy starts to fall into alignment before the song even starts in the morning; his body alignment is to stand up straighter (since he has more self-worth), he feels more powerful and his body starts to come to life with the dancing. The doctor's ritual is beginning to create more self-worth for him; he is starting his day well and aligned.

It is important to find several rituals that you will partake in every day. Create two or three rituals that support what you want to manifest. Like the doctor, find something that helps you tap into the energy and the feeling of what you wish to manifest and then experience that every day. The more rituals you have or the more times you repeat them the more the energy of what you want to manifest will start to grow and then manifest.

Don't forget – the most important part is not falling into your ego-based auto pilot personality. Your ego has rituals and habits too! And they don't serve you and work deliberately against change in your life. In order to manifest in life, we must have change. After all, receiving what you want is a change because you go from not having it to having it!

Create your rituals and share them!

An example of a ritual:

Here is an example of a student in Kalyn's class designing a ritual.

Bill: I have some real estate books from the Santa Fe area, so what I plan on doing is to put a photo of houses or businesses in a collage everyday.......I also feel music is great for opening up my feeling body which will connect me more to Self so I plan on looking for a song I can play everyday to help bring me home........

Kalyn: Great ideas, Bill. Another ritual you could create is to "practice" selling your house every day, if you want to move. You could sign a document every day that is the closing papers for the house. You can also imagine details about the closing.

Rose: I started my ritual this morning. I began by connecting to my desire to have a relationship and then I connected to my energy of BEing a loving and caring partner. I created a music mix of songs that open my FEELING BODY and help me to focus on the energy. I have also started cleaning out my house. I am creating my space in a new way that invites another person in to peace, love, relaxation and fun. I want my surroundings to remind me all the time of my desire and the energy of creating it. I'm getting rid of anything that doesn't add. I once had a writing teacher who told the class that if it doesn't add, it subtracts. And that is my mantra for creating my space.

Luther: Kalyn, I want to manifest a new job and an increase in pay. So, every morning my ritual is going to be to look in the paper and then practice interviewing the company to see if they are what I want.

Also, I'd like to be creative about this, like you said. So, I'm going to play with making new business cards for my new position. I'll put different information on it every day, like what I want my title to be, how much I'll be paid, how much I'll travel.

I feel good about this and more comfortable knowing that I will get a new job. I also feel more comfortable because I feel like I'm doing it using the law of self. The old laws really brought me down! Thank you!

Summary

The Three Laws of Manifesting:

1. The Law of Self
    a. Connect with your deep desires to bring you deeper to your Authenticity
    b. Feel the energy of them
2. The Law of Attraction
    a. Be the energy of your deep desire
    b. Be-come the alignment of the desire in your thoughts, feelings and actions
3. The Law of Repetition
    a. Practice manifesting your desire every day
    b. Create rituals, or habitual aligned behaviors, that will attract your deep desire

"A separation from god is the only lack you need to correct. "

-Course of Miracles

Author's Note:

It is very common for people to get mislead by their ego's during this process, which George illustrates well. This is not uncommon; it is important to work more deeply to learn to remove ego from our manifesting process, as these false wants will often leave us unfulfilled. Ego desires tend to use up a lot of our time and energy, often leaving us depleted and feeling empty.

"What you want, what you deeply desire, will manifest!"
– Simon Townsen

It's true! Our deep desires are meant to come true… However you think of your creator (your Higher Self, your Soul, God, etc.), your creator wishes for your deep desires to come true! People often mislead themselves by thinking that they do not deserve to have their dreams come true, blocking their own dreams. The truth is that we are all meant to have our dreams come true, so remember this!

Love & Light,

Kalyn B. Raphael

If you wish to move deeper into manifesting and/or your personal and spiritual growth, you can learn more about manifesting and take an eworkshop at http:// http://lawsofabundance.com/ .

Testimonials

"This book has been amazing!

When I began the course, I knew that my deepest desire for years had been to find a fulfilling and meaningful career. And yet, despite my best efforts I had not attained that. Within three months of doing the lessons presented here, I had my career. Magical. Absolutely magical."

Love and Light,

Joe

"The manifesting class was in full gear for me as I watched in amazement as nearly 50 thousand dollars came into my life in excess of my regular salary."
-Troy

"Kalyn, thank you so much for this book. It gave me a different perspective on manifesting and for the first time I felt like I could do it, and I have! It is wonderful to feel like I am working with the universe and not against it, like I used to always feel! Thank you again!"

-Tara

www.ingramcontent.com/pod-product-compliance
Lightning Source LLC
Chambersburg PA
CBHW051714040426
42446CB00008B/871